# CONCRETE MIXERS

by Marlene Targ Brill

Lerner Publications Company • Minneapolis

For this book, the author talked with many people who knew about concrete and trucks. She would like to thank Lucy Klocksin; Ann Howard; and Albert Draves, who came up with the idea of putting mixers together with trucks. Dick Carione sent the history of Draves's Chain Belt company. And Dale Stempel explained how concrete is made inside trucks. Their stories turned into this book.

Text copyright © 2007 by Marlene Targ Brill

Lerner Publications Company
A division of Lerner Publishing Group
241 First Avenue North
Minneapolis, MN 55401 U.S.A.

Website address: www.lernerbooks.com

Words in **bold** type are explained in a glossary on page 30.

Library of Congress Cataloging-in-Publication Data

Brill, Marlene Targ.
    Concrete mixers / by Marlene Targ Brill.
       p.   cm. – (Pull ahead books)
    Includes index.
    ISBN-13: 978-0-8225-6011-1 (lib. bdg. : alk. paper)
    ISBN-10: 0-8225-6011-9 (lib. bdg. : alk. paper)
    1. Concrete mixers—Juvenile literature. I. Title. II. Series.
TA439.B68 2007
624.1'834—dc22                  2005017967

Manufactured in the United States of America
1 2 3 4 5 6 – JR – 12 11 10 09 08 07

Wow! What kind of truck is this?

This truck is a **concrete** mixer. But what is concrete?

Concrete starts out as a wet, lumpy mix.

The mix is made of **cement**, a gray
dust that makes concrete hard.  It is
also made of **gravel**, sand, and water.

When concrete dries, it is rock hard. People use concrete to make many things. Sidewalks are made of concrete.

# Some buildings are made of concrete.

Many roads, bridges, and dams are made of concrete. How do concrete mixers help to make them?

Concrete mixers mix concrete. They carry concrete to where it is needed. How does the truck do these jobs?

A driver takes the truck to a concrete factory.

Click! Ping! Swish! The cement, gravel, sand, and water shoot down a big slide. The slide is called a **hopper.**

The hopper reaches into the **barrel** of the truck. The inside of the barrel is called a **drum.**

The driver climbs a ladder on the side of the truck. He looks into the hopper to make sure the drum is full.

Then the driver gets back in the **cab.** What does the driver do next?

The driver turns on the engine. Whirr!
The giant mixing machine starts to run.

The big barrel holding the drum turns
around and around.

**Fins** inside the drum move in circles. The fins act like large arms. They mix the cement, gravel, sand, and water together.

Then the concrete mixer is ready to go.
Vr-rr-room! The truck rolls forward.

The giant barrel keeps spinning as the truck moves. The concrete will be ready when the truck gets to the job.

The driver parks the truck near the job.
A worker pushes a button. The button
is on the outside of the truck.

Screech! A trap door on the **chute** opens. Thick concrete slides down the chute. Workers shovel the concrete across roads or sidewalks.

They can also place it into **molds** of wood or steel. They pat it hard to squash out air bubbles.

The concrete dries in the shape of the mold.

Workers remove the mold. The concrete has hardened. What happens to the truck?

The truck is out of concrete. A worker washes the empty truck.

Then the truck goes back to the factory. It gets more cement, gravel, sand, and water. What will the concrete mixer help build next?

# Facts about Concrete Mixers

■ Around 1900, the first concrete mixers were iron drums that were turned by hand. Each drum sat on an iron frame. The frame was pulled by a team of horses.

■ By 1920, cars pulled mixers. The car and the mixer each had a different motor.

■ In the 1930s, the mixer and car became one truck with one motor.

■ Fins inside the drum need to go around 70 times to mix concrete.

■ The drum holds 32,000 pounds of concrete. That is enough to make a sidewalk that is 130 feet long, 5 feet wide, and 4 inches thick. This is the length of about five elephants standing end to end in a row.

# Parts of a Cement Mixer

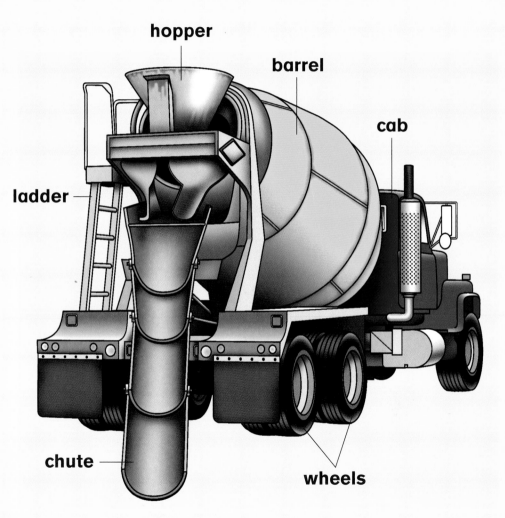

hopper

barrel

cab

ladder

chute

wheels

# Glossary

**barrel:** the large round outside part of the drum

**cab:** the part of the truck where the driver sits

**cement:** a gray dust that makes concrete hard

**chute:** a slide that carries the concrete from the drum to the wheelbarrow or the ground

**concrete:** a mix of cement, gravel, sand, and water that becomes hard when it dries

**drum:** the part of the truck where concrete is mixed

**fins:** large arms that mix the concrete inside the drum

**gravel:** small stones used to make concrete

**hopper:** a slide that shoots cement into the drum of a truck

**molds:** hollow containers that are made in a particular shape. When concrete is poured into a container, it hardens in that shape.

# More about Concrete Mixers

Check out these books and this website to find out more about concrete mixers.

## Books

Eick, Jean. *Concrete Mixers*. Eden Prairie, MN: Child's World, 1999.
  This book shows what it is like to ride inside a concrete mixer.

Katz, Bobbi. *Truck Talk: Rhymes on Wheels*. New York: Scholastic, 1997.
  This book talks about many kinds of trucks in rhyme.

Simon, Seymour. *Seymour Simon's Book of Trucks*. New York: HarperCollins, 2000.
  This book tells how different trucks are alike.

## Website

*History for Kids: Ancient Concrete*
  http://www.historyforkids.org/learn/architecture/concrete.htm
  This site shows how early people used concrete.

# Index

## Photo Acknowledgments

The photographs in this book appear courtesy of: © Todd Strand/Independent Picture Service, pp. 3, 4, 10, 19, 23, 25; © Sam Lund/Independent Picture Service, pp. 5, 15, 17, 20, 21, 24, 26; Portland Cement Association, pp. 6, 13, 14; © Royalty-Free/CORBIS, p. 7; PhotoDisc Royalty Free by Getty Images, p. 9; © H. Lange/zefa/CORBIS, p. 8; © Derek M. Allan; Travel Ink/CORBIS, p. 11; © Joseph Sohm; ChromoSohm Inc./CORBIS, p. 12; © Ernest Feland, Bobcat Company, pp. 16, 18; © Gary Moon, p. 22; © ANNEBICQUE BERNARD/CORBIS SYGMA, p. 27.

Front Cover: Photo courtesy of Mack Trucks, Inc.

# CLINGING
# SEA HORSES

by Judith Jango-Cohen

Lerner Publications Company • Minneapolis

Publisher's note: The Pull Ahead series describes animals that live in North America.
While some of the sea horses pictured in this book are not native to North American
waters, the characteristics and behaviors described in the text are typical of sea
horses throughout the world.

*This book is available in two editions:*
Library binding by Lerner Publications Company, a division of Lerner Publishing Group
Soft cover by First Avenue Editions, an imprint of Lerner Publishing Group
241 First Avenue North
Minneapolis, MN 55401 U.S.A.

Website address: www.lernerbooks.com

Words in *italic type* are explained in a glossary on page 30.

Library of Congress Cataloging-in-Publication Data

Jango-Cohen, Judith.
    Clinging sea horses / by Judith Jango-Cohen
        p.  cm.  — (Pull ahead books)
    Includes index.
    Summary: Introduces the sea horse by describing
its habitat, behaviors, and physical characteristics
including its prehensile tail.
        ISBN 0–8225–3764–8 (lib. bdg. : alk. paper)
        ISBN 0–8225–3767–2 (pbk. : alk. paper)
        1. Sea horses—Juvenile literature. [1. Sea horses.]
    I. Title. II. Series.
    QL638.S9  2001
    597'.6798—dc21                           99-050542

Manufactured in the United States of America
1 2 3 4 5 6 — JR — 06 05 04 03 02 01

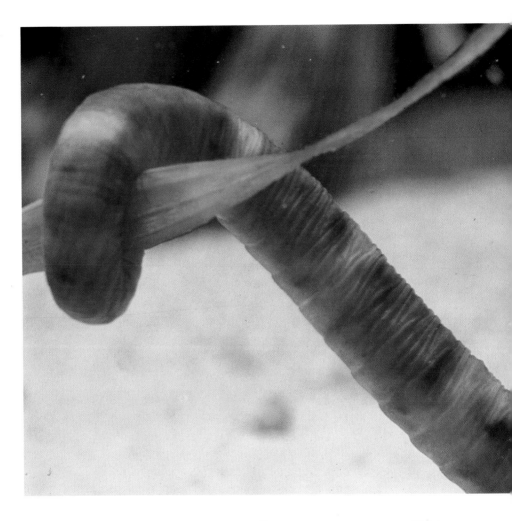

What is clinging to the sea grass?

This animal is a sea horse. Is a sea horse a horse?

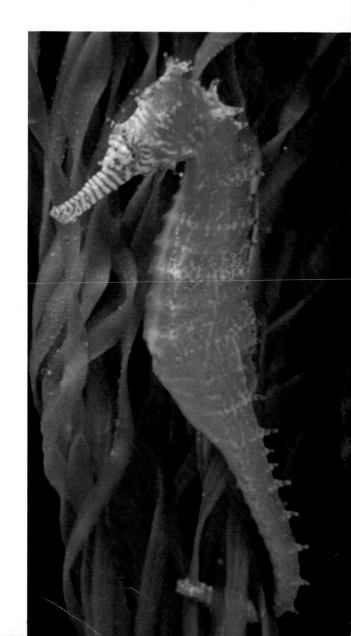

No!  A sea horse is a *fish*.
Fish live and swim in the water.

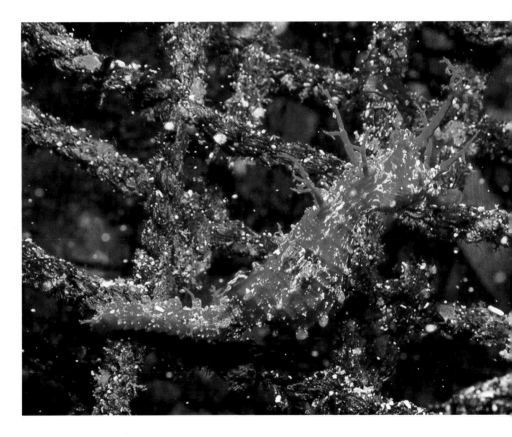

Sea horses live in the salty sea.

A sea horse can cling to things with its tail.

It clings to plant roots, *corals*, and sea grass.

Tails that grip and cling are
called *prehensile*.

Why do sea horses need
prehensile tails?

Sea horses do not swim well.

Big waves
can sweep
them away.

Clinging
keeps sea
horses safe.

Sometimes a sea horse
needs to swim.

It pushes the water with the
*fin* on its back.

To steer, a sea horse flutters
the fins on its head.

There is one fin on each side of a
sea horse's head.

Most fish swim faster than
sea horses.

Here comes a shark.
It is looking for food!

How will
the sea
horse hide?

To hide, a sea horse changes color.

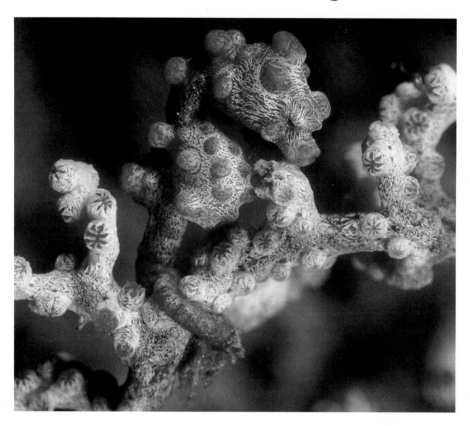

Hiding by changing color is
called *camouflage*.

How many sea horses are camouflaged here?

While a sea horse hides, it looks for food.

Sea horses eat tiny animals called *zooplankton*.

How does a sea horse catch the zooplankton that drift by?

A sea horse sucks up this sea soup
with its long *snout*.

A sea horse
also sucks
up water
with its
snout.

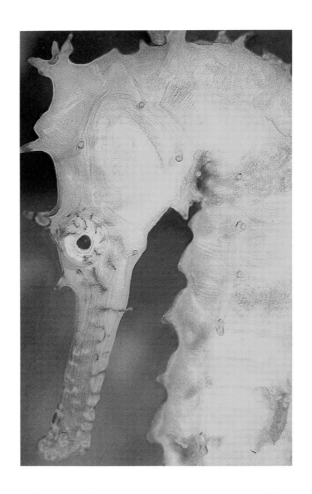

It pushes the water over its
*gills* to breathe.

Every sea horse has gills, fins, a tail, and a snout.

Only some sea horses have a *pouch*.

A pouch is a pocket for carrying eggs.

Does the mother or the father sea horse have a pouch?

Surprise!
The father
sea horse
has a
pouch.

This pouch is full of eggs.

Each egg holds a growing
sea horse.

Growing sea horses get too big for the pouch.

Then they wiggle out!

What does a sea horse do as soon as it is born?

The baby sea horse winds its tail around the first thing it finds.

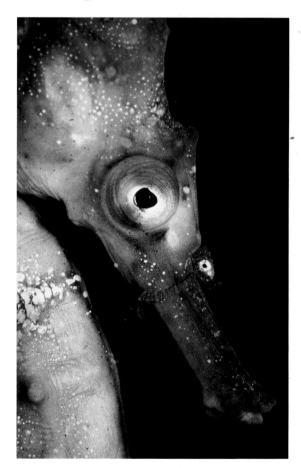

Then it holds on!

Of course!  It is a clinging sea horse.

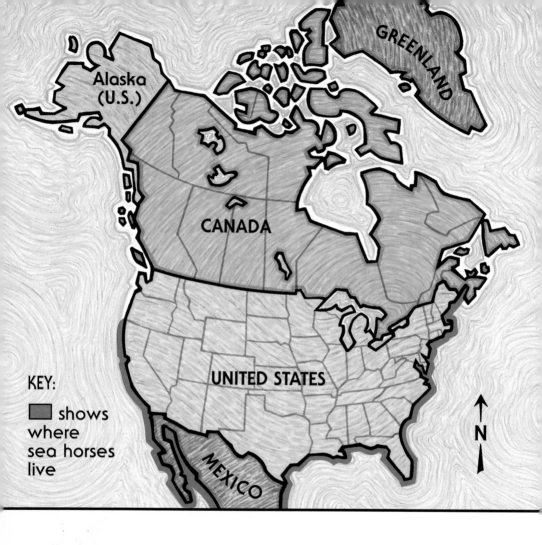

Find your state or province on this map.

Do sea horses live near you?

# Parts of a Sea Horse's Body

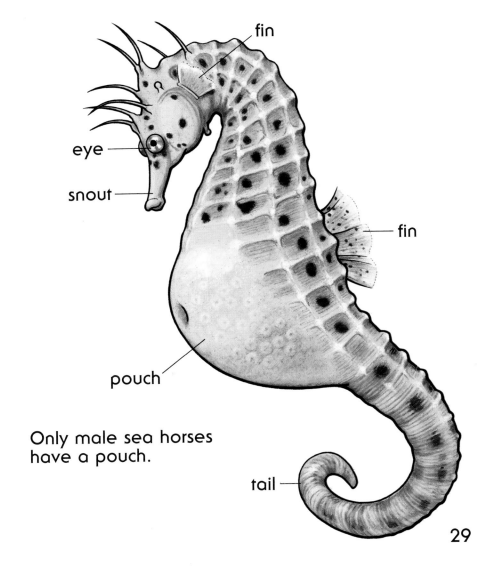

fin

eye

snout

fin

pouch

Only male sea horses
have a pouch.

tail

# Glossary

**camouflage:** hiding by blending in with the background.  One way sea horses camouflage themselves is by changing color.

**corals:** sea animals with soft, tube-shaped bodies. Most corals are tiny and live together in groups. Some grow hard skeletons outside their bodies.

**fin:** a body part that helps fish swim and steer

**fish:** an animal that lives, swims, and breathes in water

**gills:** body parts that help animals breathe underwater

**pouch:** a pocket for holding eggs

**prehensile:** able to grip and cling

**snout:** a long part on the front of an animal's head. A sea horse's snout includes its mouth.

**zooplankton:** tiny animals that drift in the water

# Hunt and Find

- **baby** sea horses on pages 24–27
- a sea horse **eating** on page 18
- sea horses **hiding** on pages 13–15
- a sea horse **hunting** on page 16
- sea horse **pouches** on pages 20–24
- sea horses **swimming** on pages 8, 10, 25

The publisher wishes to extend special thanks to our **series consultant,** Sharyn Fenwick. An elementary science-math specialist, Mrs. Fenwick was the recipient of the National Science Teachers Association 1991 Distinguished Teaching Award. In 1992, representing the state of Minnesota at the elementary level, she received the Presidential Award for Excellence in Math and Science Teaching.

# About the Author

Judith Jango-Cohen grew up in a Boston apartment with cats, turtles, and tropical fish. She loved learning about plants and animals and earned a degree in biology. For ten years she taught science to children. When her own children were born, she began working at her home in Burlington, Massachusetts, as a writer. With her husband, Eliot, and her children, Jennifer and Steven, Judith travels to many national parks. There she explores the outdoors. Her first exciting peek at sea horses, however, was indoors—at the New England Aquarium.

# Photo Acknowledgments

The photographs in this book are reproduced through the courtesy of: © Doug Perrine/Innerspace Visions, front cover, p. 6; © John G. Shedd Aquarium/Edward G. Lines Jr., pp. 3, 4, 9, 10, 11, 16, 20; © Mako Hirose/Innerspace Visions, p. 5; © Florian Ganer/Innerspace Visions, p. 7, back cover; © Denise Tackett/Tom Stack & Associates, p. 8; © Mark Conlin/Innerspace Visions, pp. 12, 23; © Larry Tackett/Tom Stack & Associates, p. 13; © Rudie Kuiter/Innerspace Visions, pp. 14, 15, 18, 21, 22, 24, 25, 26, 27, 31; © John D. Cunningham/Visuals Unlimited, p. 17; © Tom Stack/Tom Stack & Associates, p. 19. Illustrations on pp. 28, 29 by Laura Westlund.